GALAXY 9 & SAMSUNG GALAXY 9 PLUS

Copyright 2018

Michael Fox

TABLE OF CONTENTS

INTRODUCTION
CHAPTER 1 – MEET YOUR PHONE
Specifications
Unboxing the Phone
Assembling the Phone: How to Install the SIM Card.
Assembling the Phone: How to Install a Memory card.
Assembling the Phone: How to Uninstall a Memory card.

CHAPTER 2 – GETTING TO KNOW THE BASICS
How to Charge Your Phone
How to Turn Your Phone On or Off
How to Lock or Unlock Your Phone Screen
How to Create a Google Account
How to Customize Your Home Screen: Changing the Theme
How to Customize Your Home Screen: Changing the Icons

CHAPTER 3 - UNDERSTANDING YOUR PHONE
How to Use the S Pen: Removing the S Pen from the Device
How to Use the S Pen: Configuring the S Pen Settings
How to Enable and Disable the On-Screen Keyboard
How to Use Samsung Voice Input
How to Configure Your Samsung Voice Input
How to Create a Contact
How to Update an Existing Contact
How to Delete a Contact
How to Import a Contact
How to Mark Contacts as Favorites
How to Remove Contacts from Favorites
How to Add an Email Account
How to Create and Send an Email
How to create and Send a Text Message
How to Delete a Text Message
How to Enable and Use Swype to Send a Text Message
How to Copy, Delete and Replace a Text
How to Paste a Text

TABLE OF CONTENTS

How to Make a Call from the Home Screen
How to Make a Call from Your Contacts
How to Make a Call from Your Recents Call Log
How to Answer a Call
How to Put a Call on Speaker
How to View the Call Log
How to Delete Call Records
How to Block a Number
How to Connect to a Wi-Fi Network
How to Pair With a Bluetooth Device
How to Unpair from a Bluetooth Device
How to put your device on Airplane Mode
How to Enable a Mobile Network
How to Change Your Device Language

CHAPTER 4 - TAKING CONTROL OF YOUR PHONE
How to View Notifications
How to Customize Your App Notifications
How to Block App Notifications
How to Add a Calendar
How to Choose a Calendar View
Managing Events: How to Create an Event
Managing Events: How to Share an Event
Managing Events: How to Delete an Event
How to Set the Date and Time on Your Device
The Clock: How to Create an Alarm
The Clock: How to Delete an Alarm
The Clock: How to Use the Stopwatch
The Clock: How to Use the Timer
The World Clock: How to Add a City
The World Clock: How to Delete a City
How to Take a Picture
How to View a Picture
How to Record a Video
How to Play a Video

TABLE OF CONTENTS

How to Create a Music Playlist

CHAPTER 5 - PERSONALIZING YOUR PHONE
How to Personalize Your Ringtone
How to Change Your Ringtone Volume
How to Enable a Screen Saver
How to Customize Your Status Bar
How to Customize Your Screen Zoom and Font Size

CHAPTER 6 - THE WONDERFUL WORLD OF APPS
How to Access Apps on Your Phone
How to Add an App Shortcut
How to Uninstall an App
How to Organize your Apps
How to Use the App Manager
How to Manage Your Game Features

CHAPTER 7 - SECURING YOUR PHONE
How to Set a Secure Screen Lock
How to Customize Your Lock Screen
Face Recognition: How to Register a Face
Face Recognition: How to Configure Your Face Recognition
Fingerprint Scanner: How to Register a Fingerprint
Fingerprint Scanner: How to Configure Your Fingerprint Scanner
Iris Scanner: How to Register an Iris
Iris Scanner: How to Configure Your Iris Scanner

CHAPTER 8 - SAFETY PRECAUTIONS
Safety precautions & tips when the Samsung Galaxy S9 and S9+

Introduction

This manual provides detailed user-friendly information on how one should go about operating the Samsung Galaxy 9 and Samsung Galaxy 9 plus mobile device.

With this manual, you will be able to learn innovative and exciting things about your device such as mobile assembly procedures, its hardware, how to set it up, its features, its applications its settings, its connections, its battery life, its storage and its accessibility.

Chapter 1
Meet Your Phone

Specifications

The Samsung Galaxy 9 and Samsung Galaxy 9 plus is a very innovative and well- equipped device which will guide you to perform numerous functions on a daily basis. It displays a variety of features which gives its users a wide variety of options to choose from to enhance their phone function ability.

The device features a face or smile detection, auto HDR, Samsung play, geo-tagging, panorama, simultaneous 4k video recording and 9MP image recording. They comprise of a QUAD HD plus super AMOLED capacitive touchscreen display that is 5.8 and 6.2 inches in length which gives its users more space to read, watch their favorite movies, series and scroll less. On top of that, both phones enable its users to have 64 GB of memory which will enable them to store as much information as possible without having to worry about space limitation. Both devices are water resistant and dust resistant for up to 5 feet of water for up to 30 minutes which makes it even more exciting to have. For extra phone protection, the phones come with an iris scanner, fingerprint scanner, biometric authentication and a facial recognition system to protect one from being open to threats. They are also equipped with a 12 MP dual wide-angled rear camera with dual Optical Image Stabilization (OIS) and telephoto along with an 8 MP smart autofocus front camera. Unsurprisingly, both devices run on the latest edition of Android 8.0 (Oreo) and come with a Bixby assistant that responds to voice commands promptly.

Unboxing the Phone

When you open the package for your new Samsung 9 and 9 plus mobile device, you will find the following:

- ➢ The phone itself
- ➢ Micro USB connector
- ➢ USB cable
- ➢ USB power adaptor

- USB connector (USB Type-C)
- Earphone
- S Pen
- Case

Assembling the phone: How to insert the Sim Card

The first step to take to set up your mobile device is to install a **Sim** card.

To insert your Sim card into your Samsung Galaxy 9 and 9 + you must do the following:

1. Insert the ejection pin into the hold on the tray to loosen the tray
2. Pull the tray gently from the slot
3. Place the SIM on the tray facing downwards

Note Briefly: If the Sim card is inserted incorrectly, the device will fail to detect your Sim card. If this happens you are required to remove the sim card out of the slot and place it back in the slot.

Assembling the phone: How to install a Memory Card

If you wish to add more memory space to your device, you can simply install a micro SD memory card. To install this micro SD memory card, you are required to do the following:

1. Open the cover of the SIM card/memory card slot then,
2. Cautiously slide the memory card into the slot with the gold contacts face down while gently pushing it until it locks into place then,
3. Replace the memory card slot cover

Assembling the phone: How to uninstall a Memory Card

It is often safer for you to remove a Micro SD Memory Card properly in order to prevent loss of information, prevent it from being corrupted and from it being damaged. To uninstall this Micro SD Memory Card, you will be instructed to do the following:

1. From your Home screen, go to Apps and then press Settings and then press Storage then,
2. Under the heading 'SD Card', select 'Unmount SD card' and then select 'OK' then,
3. Open the SIM card/Memory card slot then,
4. Press gently on the memory card so that it pops out of the slot and then,
5. Cautiously pull the memory card out of the slot then,
6. Put back the SIM card/Memory card slot cover

Chapter 2
Getting To Know the Basics

How to charge your phone

The Samsung Galaxy 9 and 9 plus is powered by a rechargeable standard Li-Ion battery which operates at 3,000 and 3,500 mAh .They come with a USB wall charger (USB cable and charging head) to charge the battery from any standard outlet. Before using your device for the first time, the battery must be fully charged after which you can use the device while charging. To charge your Samsung Galaxy 9 and 9 plus mobile device, you must:

1. Insert the USB cable into the device's Accessory port (USB charger), then,

2. Insert the USB cable into the charging head and then,

3. Plug in the charging head into the standard outlet after which,

4. Once charging is complete, unplug the charging head from the standard outlet and remove the USB cable from the device.

When this happens you will notice that your phone screen will become dim or dark. This will help to conserve what is left of the battery power. Note that it is completely normal for your mobile device and the charger to become hot when charging, but it will not affect the lifespan of the battery.

How to turn your Device On /Off

To turn on your Samsung Galaxy 9 and 9+ mobile devices, you must do the following:

1. Press and hold the Power/Lock key until the device's screen lights up.

To turn off your Samsung Galaxy 9 and 9 + mobile device, you must do the following:

1. Press and hold the Power/Lock key until prompted, then
2. At the prompt, tap the power off by selecting **'OK'** and then,
3. Confirm if prompted again

How to Lock / Unlock your Phone Screen

Your Samsung Galaxy 9 and 9 plus mobile device will automatically lock whenever the screen has timed out. To lock your device you must:

1. Press the **Power key** button

You could also unlock your device by:

1. Pressing the Power button or double tap Home
2. Swiping your finger across the screen
3. Entering your password

How to Create a Google Account

In order for the device to fully utilize its Android features, it is required that a Google account must be set up. To set up a Google account on your Samsung Galaxy 9 and 9 + device you must:

1. From the Home screen touch **'Apps'**.

2. Touch **'Settings'**.

3. Touch **'Accounts'** (you may need to touch the General tab first if your settings are in tabs).

4. Touch **'Add account'**.

5. Touch **'Google'**.

6. Follow the steps to enter the email address and password for your Google/Gmail account.

How to Customize your Home Screen: Changing the Theme

You can change the background (wallpaper) on your smart device. Your device will include a choice of wallpapers, or you can choose your own image to use as a wallpaper. You must:

1. Go to one of the Home Screen panels then,

2. Touch and hold down on the screen or use the S Pen to touch and hold down on the screen until the pop-up for the Home Screen displays or then,

3. Tap on **'View All'** to see all available wallpaper pictures then,

4. Select '**Set as Wallpaper**' to select the wallpaper picture you want and,

5. Select **'OK'**

How to Customize Your Home Screen: Changing the Icons

To customize your Home Screen by changing the Icons you must do the following:

1. On your Home Screen, long press the screen then,

2. Tap on '**Wallpaper and Themes**' and select '**Icons**' then,

3. Tap on a set of Icons to preview and download them to My Icons then,

4. Select '**View All**' to see all the downloaded icons then,

5. Tap on an icon and then select '**Apply**' to apply the icon set you selected.

Chapter 3
Understanding Your Phone

How to Use the S Pen: Removing the S Pen from the Device

For your convenience, the Samsung Galaxy 9 and 9 + comes with a handy tool called the S Pen. In order for you to utilize this tool, you must first know how and where to locate it and how to use it. The S Pen is located at the lower right- hand corner of the device, to remove it you must:

1. Use a sharp object or your fingernail to gently pull on the end of the S Pen so as to pull it from the device then,

2. Gently pull the S Pen out of the device.

How to use the S Pen: Configuring the S Pen Settings

To configure the settings for the S Pen to suit the preference you must:

1. From the Home screen, swipe to access your Apps then,

2. Go to '**Settings**' then,

3. Select '**S Pen**' option to configure settings such as screen off the memo, direct pen input, pointer, air view, shortcuts, floating icons, sounds, vibrations, alarms and power saver.

How to customize the Samsung Keyboard

To customize your Samsung Keyboard to suit the preference you must:

1. Swipe upwards on the Home screen to access your apps then,

2. Go to '**Settings**' then,

3. Go to '**Language and Input'** then,

4. Go to '**On-Screen Keyboard** then,

5. Go to 'Samsung Keyboard' for options such as Languages and Types and Predictive Texts.

How to Enable and Disable the On-Screen Keyboard

You can enable and disable the on-screen keyboard whenever you like, to do so you:

1. Swipe the Home screen upwards to access apps then,

2. Go to '**Settings**' then,

3. Go to '**Language and Input**' then,

4. Tap on '**On-screen Keyboard**' then,

5. Go to '**Manage Keyboards**' then,

6. Tap on whichever keyboard you want to enable/disable.

How to Use Samsung Voice Input

You have options for speaking or entering a text by typing with the Samsung Voice Input.

To have access to this voice input you must do the following:

1. You may need to touch and hold **'Options'** (left of the Spacebar)

2. Tap **'Voice Input'** on the Samsung keyboard

3. Speak your text

How to Configure Your Samsung Voice Input

To configure the settings of your Samsung Voice Input you should:

1. Go on the Home screen
2. Go to '**Settings**'
3. Tap '**Language and Input**'
4. Go to '**On-Screen Keyboard**
5. Go to '**Samsung Voice Input**' for options such as hiding offensive words, keyboard language and voice input language

How to Create a Contact

To create a contact in your mobile device you must:

1. Tap '**Apps**'
2. Go to Home Screen
3. Tap Create '**Contact** '
4. After you store the information tap ' **Save**'

How to update an Existing Contact

To update an existing contact you should:

1. Select **'Apps'** from your home screen
2. Go to **'Contacts'**
3. Select a contact list to view the information
4. Tap on **'Edit'**
5. Enter the information that you want to change
6. After you are done with entering the information select **'Save'**

How to Delete a Contact

1. Touch **'Apps'**
2. Scroll and touch **'Contacts'**
3. Scroll and touch the contact you want to delete
4. Select **'Delete'**
5. Select **'Ok'** to confirm

How to Import a Contact

To import a contact from an installed memory card to your device you must:

1. Swipe upwards on the Home screen to access your apps then,
2. Go to **'Contacts'**
3. Select **'More Options'**
4. Select **'Manage Contacts'**
5. Tap on **'Import/Export Contacts'**

How to Mark Contacts as Favorites

These contacts are automatically assigned at the top of your contact list.

1. Launch the **'Phone app'** on your device and find the contact you'd like to set as a favourite

2. Open their contact card and tap the '**Star icon**' at the top of the card. This adds them to the **Favourites** tab

3. Now simply open the '**Favourites tab**' and you should see them added

4. A yellow star will pop up which indicates that the contact was added as favorites

How to Remove Contacts from Favorites

To remove a contact from your favorites list you should:

1. From home, tap '**Apps**'
2. Tap on '**Contacts**'
3. Tap on the contact that you want to remove
4. Then tap '**Details**'
5. Select '**Remove from favorites**'
6. The yellow star will dim to signify that the contact no longer exists as favorites

How to Add an Email Account

Having an email is a fast and reliable way of retrieving messages to keep you updated on your mobile device.

Here are a few ways in which you can create an email:

1. Swipe upwards on your Home screen
2. Go to **'Settings'** then,
3. Select **'Accounts'**
4. Then select **'Add accounts'** then,
5. Tap **'Email'** to create an account

How to Create and Send an Email

The email app is a reliable way of creating and sending an email. For you to create and send an email you should:

1. Swipe upwards on your Home screen
2. Tap on **'Email'** then,
3. Select **'Compose'** then,
4. Tap on **'To'** row to add an email or select from contacts to select a contact then,

5. Tap on **'Subject'** and write something to enter your text then,
6. Tap on **'Attach files'** to add files, videos and other attachments if required then,
7. Tap on '**Select**' to send your email

How to create and Send a Text Message

You can send and create text messages by accessing the Message app. To do so, you are required to:

1. From the home screen, select **'Messaging'**
2. Select '**New message**' (located at the top of the display)
3. From the '**To field**,' enter a number consisting of 7 digits or more or a contact name
4. From the Type to '**Compose field**', enter a message
5. Select **'Send'** to send your message

How to Delete a Text Message

You have the opportunity of deleting text messages that you have received if you no longer see the need of keeping them in storage. You do this by:

1. From the home screen, tap **'Messaging'**
2. Tap and hold the preferred **'Message thread'**
3. Tap **'Delete'**
4. Select **'Ok'** to confirm

How to Enable and Use Swype to Send a Text Message

Swype is a virtual keyboard for touchscreen, smartphones, and tablets that enables its users to enter a text by sliding their fingers from letter to letter while lifting your fingers in between each word. In order for you to have access to this feature, you must change your default keyboard settings. To enable this, you must:

1. From a screen where you enter text, touch and drag down the notifications area then,
2. Tap on '**Choose Input Method**' then,
3. Tap on the '**Swype button**' that will turn green then,
4. The Swype keyboard will be shown then,
5. Draw a path over the letters you want with your fingers or with your S Pen to enter your text

How to Copy, Delete and Replace a Text

To copy, delete and replace a text you will need to:

1. Touch and hold the screen area containing the selected text until the text select is shown.
   - Note that the text will need to be selectable. For example, you may not be able to select text shown as part of an image.

2. Adjust the selected area by touching and dragging the anchors' icons at either end of the selected text.
   - Any selected text will appear highlighted.
3. The following options are available after you select text. You may need to swipe on the bar to view additional options and, depending on the app you're in, not all these options may be available.
   - Touch Select all to highlight all the visible text on the page.
   - Cut (to remove the selected text)
   - Touch Copy to make the selected area available for pasting into other apps.

How to Paste a Text

For you to paste a text which you have previously copied you should:

1. Touch the text at whichever point you wish to paste the copied text then,
2. Touch and hold the cursor until a pop-up is displayed then,
3. Tap on 'Paste' in the pop-up

How to make a call from the Home Screen

You will be able to make calls from your contact list by following these steps:

1. On the Home screen tap on '**Phone**' to bring the dialer up then,

2. Enter the number you want to call on the keypad then,

3. Tap on '**Call**' to dial the number and make the call

How to make a call from Your Contacts

1. Go to your Home screen menu and access your contacts app then,

2. Go to your '**Contacts**' section then,

3. Swipe your fingers across the contact that you want to call

How to make a call from your recent Call Log

Once a call has been sent out, it is automatically stored in your call log. You can access your call log by:

1. Swipe the Home screen upwards to access your app then,
2. Go to '**Phone**' then,
3. Go to '**Recents**' which will display a list of all your recent calls then,
4. Tap on the contact you want to call then,
5. Tap on '**Call**' to call the selected contact

How to answer a Call

When you receive an incoming call your phone automatically rings or vibrates depending on the profile which you set-up your phone on, and it displays the caller's information on the screen.

To answer an incoming call you are required to do the following:

1. Swipe your finger to the right of the screen to answer the call or

2. Swipe your finger to the left of the screen to reject the call.

After you are through with your conversation, you tap on the '**End**' button to end the call.

How to put a call on Speaker

If you are too busy to come to the phone or to hold it in your hand, there are alternatives for this problem such as a speaker and a Bluetooth headset.

To put a call on the speaker you can simply:

1. Tap on **'Speaker'** to put the call on hands- free OR

2. You can tap on **'Bluetooth'** to hear the call using a Bluetooth headset even if you are a bit distant from your phone

How to View the Call Log

Your call log automatically stores calls you have missed, received and dialled.

To view your call log you can do the following:

1. Go to your Home screen and tap on **'Phone'**
2. Go to **'Recents'** section
3. Here you will see a list of recent contacts { received, missed and dialled }

How to Delete Call Records

You are able to delete call records from your call log entries. You can do so by:

1. Go to your Home screen and Tap on **'Phone'**
2. Go to the **'Recents'** section

Here you will see a list of previous calls {received, dialled and missed calls}

3. Touch and hold down on the call log entry which you want to delete

4. Tap on the **'Delete'** button to delete your data

How to Block a Number

If you no longer want to be contacted by someone, you can simply block that person by adding that person to the block list section.

To block a number from calling you, you can do the following:

1. From your Home screen tap on **'Phone'**
2. Tap **'Recents'** or **'Contacts'**
3. You will see a list of all your recent calls (dialled, missed, received) then,
4. Touch and hold down on the number you want block then,
5. Tap on '**Details'** then,
6. Tap on '**More Options**' then,
7. Select '**Block number'** then,
8. Select '**OK'** to confirm

How to Connect To a Wi-Fi Network

Activate the Wi-Fi feature to connect to a Wi-Fi network and access the Internet or other network devices. You can connect to a Network by following these steps:

1. Tap on the home screen button
2. Go to **'Settings'**
3. **Go to 'Wi-Fi'**
4. Tap on **On/ Off** to turn the Wi-Fi on
5. Select the Network that you want to connect to
6. If Network connection is secured it will automatically ask you to enter a password
7. If Network is not safe it will automatically give you access to the network

How to Pair With a Bluetooth Device

The pairing of Bluetooth devices enables you to connect to devices and exchange information overshot distances. To pair with a Bluetooth device you should:

1. Go to **'Settings'**
2. Tap on **'Bluetooth'**
3. Tap on **On/Off** to activate your Bluetooth
4. Select '**Scan**' to scan for nearby Bluetooth devices then
5. Tap on the name of the device that you want to pair /connect with
6. Your device will automatically start pairing with the device which you have selected

How to unpair from a Bluetooth Device

You can unpair your Bluetooth device if the service is no longer needed. You can unpair your device by:

1. Swipe upwards on the Home screen to access your App
2. Go to '**Settings**' then,
3. Got to '**Bluetooth**' then
4. Tap on **On/Off** to turn on your Bluetooth then,

5. Tap on '**Settings**' located next to the paired device then,
6. Tap on '**Unpair**' to delete the paired device

How to put your device on Airplane Mode

When your mobile device is put in Airplane mode, your mobile device automatically becomes disconnected from all networks. To enable or disable Airplane Mode you:

1. Go to your Home screen apps
2. Go to **settings**
3. Go to **Airplane Mode**
4. Tap on **On/Off** to enable/ disable Airplane mode

How to Enable a Mobile Network

To activate a Mobile Network you should do the following:

1. From the home screen, tap Apps.

2. Tap **Settings**

3. Scroll to and tap **More networks**

4. Tap **Mobile networks.**

5. Tap **Mobile data.**

6. Tap **OK** if prompted

How to Change Your Device Language

To change your device's language you:

1. Go to the Home screen to access your apps
2. Go to '**Settings**'
3. Go to '**Language and Input**'
4. Go to '**Language**
5. Tap on '**Add Language**' and choose a language from the list
6. Touch and hold down on '**Move**' beside the language
7. Drag the selected language to the top of the list to set it as the device language

8. Tap on **'Apply'** to apply the selected language

Chapter 4
Taking Control of your Phone

How to View Notifications

With your Samsung Galaxy 9 and 9 plus mobile device, you will be able to receive new notifications, such as messages or missed calls. Indicator icons appear on the status bar.

To have access to your notifications you:

1. Drag the status bar downwards which will display the notification status bar
2. Swipe your finger down the list to view your notifications
3. If you wish to open a notification then tap on it or
4. To clear a notification, drag the notification left or right or
5. To clear all notifications tap on 'Clear all'.

How to Customize your App Notifications

1. From the Home screen, touch Apps.
2. Navigate to Settings
3. Go to Notifications
4. Touch the app to change the notification setting
5. Choose from the following:
   - Touch an app to hiding from the Lock screen
   - Touch the slider to turn on Hide on lock screen
   - All notifications

How to Block App Notifications

You can block app notifications for the following:

1. Swipe upwards on the Home screen to access your apps
2. Go to 'Settings'
3. Go to 'Notifications'

4. Tap on 'On/Off' beside the app to disable notifications or
5. Tap on 'All' to disable notifications

How to Add a Calendar

You can add a calendar app to your calendar and you do this by following these few steps:

1. Swipe upwards on the Home screen to get access to your apps
2. Tap on 'Calendar'
3. Tap on 'More Options'
4. Tap on 'Manage Calendars'
5. Go to 'Add Account' and select the account type that you wish to desire
6. Enter your required account information

How to Choose a Calendar View

Your calendar view should be something that matches your personality. To choose a calendar you:

1. Swipe upwards on the Home screen to get full access to your apps
2. Tap on 'Calendar'
3. Go to 'View'
4. Select from the options given (Week, Month ,Year ,Days and Tasks)
5. Tap on 'Today' to return to the current date

Managing Events: How to create an event

With your newly improved mobile device, you will be able to create events that will last a lifetime. You create an event by:

1. Swipe upwards on the Home screen to access your apps

2. Tap on 'Calendar'
3. Go to 'Add' to add the event that you want
4. Enter the information for that event
5. Tap on 'Save' to save the event which you have created

Managing Events: How to share an Event

To share an event you:

1. Swipe upwards on the Home screen to access your apps
2. Tap on 'Calendar'
3. Tap on the event that you want to share
4. Tap on 'Share' to choose a shared method
5. Follow the prompts that come afterward

Managing Events: How to Delete an Event

You can get rid of an event that you no longer need. You delete an event by doing the following:

1. Swipe upwards on the Home screen to access your apps
2. Go to 'Calendar'
3. Go to 'Event' so you can edit it
4. Select 'Delete'
5. Tap 'Ok' for confirmation

How to Set the Date and Time on Your Device

You set the date and time on your device by:

1. Swipe the Home screen upwards to access apps
2. Go to 'Settings'
3. Go to 'Date and Time' then,
4. Select your time format from the following options :
    a. Automatic date and time'

b. Use 24-hour format

The Clock: How to Create an Alarm

You can set your alarm clock for an event or for a simple reminder to do something. To create an alarm you:

1. Swipe upwards on the Home screen to access your apps
2. Tap on 'Clock'
3. Select 'Alarm clock'
4. Set an alarm time, select the days on which the alarm will repeat, and then set other various alarm options
5. Tap 'Save'
- The saved alarm is added to the alarms list

The Clock: How to Delete an Alarm

You can delete an alarm that you created. To do this you:

1. Tap on 'Clock'
2. select alarms that you want to delete from the list
3. Tap on 'Done'

The Clock: How to use the Stopwatch

This device is used for timing one's self.

To use the stopwatch you:

1. Swipe upwards on the Home screen to access your apps then,
2. Tap on 'Clock' then,
3. Go to 'Stopwatch' then,
4. Select from the following options:
   - Start
   - Stop
   - Resume
   - Lap
   - Reset

The Clock: How to use the Timer

The timer is a good way to keep you on track.

To use the Timer you do the following:

1. Tap on 'Clock' then,
2. Go to 'Timer' then,
3. Use your keypad to tap on the seconds, minutes and hours to set the length of the timer then,
4. Select from the following options:
   a. Start
   b. Pause
   c. Resume
   d. Cancel

The World Clock: How to Add a City

You can view the current times of different countries around the world with the world clock. To do so with the world clock screen you:

1. Swipe upwards on the Home screen to access your apps then,
2. Select 'Clock' then,
3. Select 'World Clock' then,
4. Tap on 'Add City' then,
5. Select 'Search' and enter the name of the city you want to add then,
6. Tap on the city name and select 'Add'

The World Clock: How to Delete a City

To delete a city you do the following:

1. Select the ' Clock' app from your Home screen
2. Tap on the 'World Clock' tab. It's the globe in the bottom left corner of your screen
3. Swipe left on the city you wish to remove
4. Tap the 'Delete' button to the right of the city

How to Take a Picture

You can use your device to take pictures by using its front or rear camera. To take a picture you:

1. Swipe the Home screen
2. Go to 'Camera' then,
3. Use your display screen as a viewfinder by pointing the camera at the subject then,
4. Compose your picture by using the following options:
    a. Add shooting mode
    b. Switch between front and rear camera
    c. Add a camera setting
    d. Add an effects filter
5. Then you tap on 'Take Picture' to snap your picture

How to View a Picture

Your picture is automatically stored in your device after it was taken. You review a picture by doing the following:

1. Go to the Home screen upwards to access your apps

2. Go to '**Gallery**' then,
3. Go to '**Pictures**' or '**Albums**' or '**Stories**' to select the way your items are shown then,
4. Tap on a picture to view it

How to Record a Video

This device can be used to produce high-quality videos with its great capacity of a 12 Mega Pixel camera.

To record a video with your device, you:

1. Go to '**Camera**' then,
2. Use your display screen to aim the camera at the target then,
3. Tap on **'Record'** to start recording your video the,
4. While recording, you have the following options available:
   - Pausing the video
   - Resuming the video
5. Then when you have finished recording your video, tap on '**Stop**' to stop recording the video

How to Play a Video

To view your saved videos, you:

1. Swipe the Home screen upwards to access apps then,
2. Go to '**Gallery**' then,
3. Go to '**Videos**' to open the folder where your videos are stored then,
4. Tap on a video to view it then
5. Tap on '**Play Video**' to play the video

How to Create a Music Playlist

To create a music playlist, you:

1. Swipe the Home screen upwards to access apps then,
1. Go to '**Music Player**' then,
2. Tap on '**Create a Playlist**' then,
3. Select use the keyboard to enter a name for the playlist.

CHAPTER 5
Personalizing your Phone

How to Personalize your Ringtone

Use a ringtone that suits your personality. You can personalize your ringtone by doing the following:

1. Swipe upwards on the Home screen to access your apps then,
2. Go to '**Settings**' then,
3. Go to '**Sounds and Vibrations**' then,
4. Go to '**Ringtone**' then,
5. Tap on any ringtone to hear a preview of how it sounds then,
6. Select the ringtone of your choice or,
7. Tap on '**Add from Phone'** to select an audio file as your ringtone

How to Change Your Ringtone Volume

To change your ringtone volume you:

1. From the home screen, swipe down on the Status bar
2. Tap the Settings icon
3. Scroll to and tap Sounds and vibration
4. Tap Volume
5. Adjust the Notifications slider, then tap the Back key

How to Enable a Screen Saver

The screensaver is what controls what is being displayed on your screen. To enable a screen saver, you:

1. Swipe the Home screen upwards to access apps
2. Go to '**Settings**'
3. Go to '**Display**'
4. Select '**Screen saver**'

5. Tap on '**On/Off**' to enable screen saver (you have the option of display colors or photos).

How to Customize Your Status Bar

You can modify the display options on your status bar. You do this by:

1. Go to '**Settings**' then,
2. Go to '**Display**' then,
3. Select '**Status Bar**' then,
4. Select from the following options how you wish to display your status bar:
    - Show battery percentage
    - Show recent notifications
    - Use 12- hour format
    - Automatically start

How to Customize Your Screen Zoom and Font Size

To adjust your font size and screen zoom level, you should:

1. Swipe the Home screen upwards to access apps
2. Go to '**Settings**' then,
3. Go to '**Display**' then,
4. Select **'Zoom and Font'** then,
5. Drag the font size slider to change the text size or
6. Drag the screen zoom slider to change the zoom level or
7. Tap on a specific font to select it
8. Select **'Apply'** to confirm

CHAPTER 6
The Wonderful World of Apps

How to Access Apps on Your Phone

An app is a type of software that allows you to perform specific tasks. To have full access to your apps, you must:

1. Swipe the Home screen upwards to access apps
2. Touch the app's shortcut to launch it
3. Touch Home to return to the main Home screen

How to Add an App Shortcut

To create a shortcut for your app, you:

1. From the Home screen, tap the Menu button
2. Tap the Add button
3. Tap Shortcuts
4. Tap the Shortcuts selection you want

How to Uninstall an App

To uninstall an app from your mobile device, you:

1. Tap the Menu key and then tap **Settings**
2. Select **More** and tap on Application manager
3. **Swipe across to All**
4. Tap on the app which you wish to remove
5. Tap on **Uninstall**
6. Tap **Ok**

Once the application has been removed tap **Ok**

How to Organize your Apps

To properly organize your apps one should:

1. Swipe the Home screen upwards to access apps
2. Touch and hold down on an app shortcut or folder
3. Drag the app shortcut to a new location to arrange your Apps

To arrange your Apps in alphabetical order you must:

1. Swipe the Home screen upwards to access apps then,
2. Go to '**More Options**' then,
3. Go to '**Sort**' then,
4. Tap on '**Alphabetical order**'

How to Use the App Manager

To use an App Manager you must be able to do the following:

1. Launch the **Settings** app from your Home screen or from the app drawer.
2. Tap **Applications**.
3. Tap **Application manager**.

4. Tap the **app** you'd like to disable.

5. Tap the **Force Stop** button if it is highlighted. If it isn't, then the app isn't running.

6. Tap **Force Stop** in the pop-up. You will be warned that force stopping may cause errors, so make sure you aren't using any other apps that rely on the one you're stopping.

How to Manage your Game Features

All of your games can be listed in one place altogether. To do this, you should:

1. Swipe the Home screen upwards to access the apps
2. Go to '**Settings**'
3. Go to '**Advanced Features**'
4. Tap on '**Games**'
5. Select **'Game Launcher'**

Chapter 7
Securing your Phone

How to set a secure Screen Lock

You can secure your mobile device through a security protected system that you trust to give you the best coverage as possible. To help you secure your device you must:

1. Swipe the Home screen upwards to access apps
2. Go to '**Settings**'
3. Go to '**Lock Screen and Security**'
4. Tap on '**Screen Lock Type**'
5. Select the type of screen lock you want whether it be a PIN, password or pattern
6. Tap on '**On/Off**' to enable the selected screen lock
7. Tap **Done** when you are complete

How to Customize your Lock Screen

You can personalize your lock screen to suit your preference. To customize your lock screen, you:

1. Swipe the Home screen upwards to access apps then,
2. Go to '**Settings**' then,
3. Go to '**Lock Screen and Security**' then,
4. Select from the following options the one you want to be displayed on your lock screen:
    a. App shortcuts
    b. Notifications
    c. Information and face widgets

Face Recognition: How to Register a Face

A facial recognition system is a computer application capable of identifying or verifying a person from a digital image or a video frame from a video source. For you to go about registering your facial recognition you must first enter a PIN, Password or a Pattern. To register you:

1. Swipe upwards on your Home screen and access apps
2. Open the **'Settings'** menu
3. Go to '**Lock screen and security**'
4. Tap on **'Face Recognition'**
5. Tap the option that says **'Turn On'** to enable the feature

Face Recognition: How to Configure Your Face Recognition

To unlock your Samsung Galaxy 9 and Samsung Galaxy 9+ you should:

1. Go to your Home screen menu
2. Go to '**Settings**'
3. Go to '**Lock screen and security**'
4. Go to **'Face Recognition'**
5. Follow the instructions given

Fingerprint Scanner: How to Register a Fingerprint

The Fingerprint scanner feature can be used for entering passwords on your mobile device. To do this, you must:

1. Go to your Home screen menu
2. Go to '**Settings**' menu
3. Go to '**Lock screen and security**'
4. Tap **'Fingerprint Scanner'**
5. Tap **'Add fingerprint'**
6. Follow the instructions given
7. Press **'Done'**

Fingerprint Scanner: How to Configure Your Fingerprint Scanner

To configure your Fingerprint to unlock your Samsung Galaxy 9 and 9 plus mobile device, you must:

1. Go to Home screen menu

2. Tap on **'Settings'**
3. Tap on **'Lock screen and Security'**
4. Tap on **'Fingerprint Scanner'**
5. Choose your pick from the series of options given

Iris Scanner: How to Register an Iris

This feature allows you to have access to your phone by using the IRIS.

To register an Iris you must:

1. On the Apps screen, tap **Settings**
2. Tap **Lock screen and security**
3. Tap **Iris Scanner**
4. Select **Next**
5. Choose from the series of options that pops up

Iris Scanner: How to Configure Your Iris Scanner

This feature scans your eyes and will open your device only to them. It will work for you, and only you.

To configure your Iris Scanner on your mobile device you must:

1. On the Apps screen, **tap Settings**
2. Go to '**Lock screen and security**'
3. Tap on '**Iris Scanner**'
4. Enter your PIN, password, or pattern if asked
5. If your iris is not registered, the phone will walk you through the process of doing so
6. To use your iris to unlock the phone, ensure **'Iris Unlock'** is toggled on.

Chapter 8
Safety Precautions

Safety precautions when using the Samsung Galaxy 9 and 9 Plus

1. Get rid of all protective plastic film before using the device
2. Do not try to open or pull apart the phone, adapter, or accessories.
3. Do not pound or pierce the phone, adapter, or accessories.
4. Do not expose the phone or adapter to flames that are open or throw them away in fire or water.
5. Do not try to dry a wet adapter in an oven, microwave, or dryer as this may lead to further damage.

Safety tips for Samsung Galaxy 9 and 9 Plus

Before cleaning the phone, ensure that it is unplugged.

1. Unplug the phone during lightning storms, or when not in use for long a period of time.
2. Clean the device and accessories with a clean, soft, and dry cloth.
3. Chemicals should not be used to clean the phone or accessories.
4. Do not speak on the device while it is being charged, especially if becomes overheated.

Made in the USA
San Bernardino, CA
05 April 2019